DISCOVER AMERICA

WEST VIRGINIA

Val Lawton

MEDIA ENHANCED BOOKS
AV2 BY WEIGL
ADDED VALUE · AUDIO VISUAL

www.av2books.com

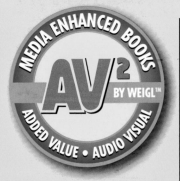

AV² provides enriched content that supplements and complements this book. Weigl's AV² books strive to create inspired learning and engage young minds in a total learning experience.

Go to **www.av2books.com**, and enter this book's unique code.

BOOK CODE

R 9 3 2 6 5 5

AV² by Weigl brings you media enhanced books that support active learning.

Your AV² Media Enhanced books come alive with...

Audio
Listen to sections of the book read aloud.

Key Words
Study vocabulary, and complete a matching word activity.

Video
Watch informative video clips.

Quizzes
Test your knowledge.

Embedded Weblinks
Gain additional information for research.

Slide Show
View images and captions, and prepare a presentation.

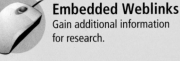

Try This!
Complete activities and hands-on experiments.

... and much, much more!

Published by AV² by Weigl
350 5th Avenue, 59th Floor
New York, NY 10118
Website: www.av2books.com

Library of Congress Cataloging-in-Publication Data
Names: Lawton, Val, author.
Title: West Virginia : the Mountain State / Val Lawton.
Description: New York, NY : AV2 by Weigl, [2016] | Series: Discover America |
  Includes index.
Identifiers: LCCN 2015048068 (print) | LCCN 2015048341 (ebook) | ISBN
  9781489649621 (hard cover : alk. paper) | ISBN 9781489649638 (soft cover :
  alk. paper) | ISBN 9781489649645 (Multi-User eBook)
Subjects: LCSH: West Virginia--Juvenile literature.
Classification: LCC F241.3 .L393 2016 (print) | LCC F241.3 (ebook) | DDC 975.4--dc23
LC record available at http://lccn.loc.gov/2015048068

Printed in the United States of America, in Brainerd, Minnesota
1 2 3 4 5 6 7 8 9 20 19 18 17 16

082016
210716

Project Coordinator Heather Kissock
Art Director Terry Paulhus

Photo Credits
Every reasonable effort has been made to trace ownership and to obtain permission to reprint copyright material. The publisher would be pleased to have any errors or omissions brought to their attention so that they may be corrected in subsequent printings. The publisher acknowledges Getty Images, iStock Images, and Alamy as its primary image suppliers for this title.

WEST VIRGINIA

Contents

AV² Book Code 2
Discover West Virginia 4

THE LAND
Beginnings 6
Where is West Virginia? 8
Land Features 10
Climate 12
Nature's Resources 14
Vegetation 16
Wildlife 18

ECONOMY
Tourism 20
Primary Industries 22
Goods and Services 24

HISTORY
Native Americans 26
Exploring the Land 28
The First Settlers 30
History Makers 32

CULTURE
The People Today 34
State Government 36
Celebrating Culture 38
Arts and Entertainment 40
Sports and Recreation 42

Get to Know West Virginia 44
Brain Teasers 46
Key Words/Index 47
Log on to www.av2books.com 48

STATE TREE
Sugar Maple

STATE BIRD
Northern Cardinal

STATE FLOWER
Rhododendron

STATE FLAG
West Virginia

STATE ANIMAL
Black Bear

STATE SEAL
West Virginia

Nicknames
The Mountain State

Song
"This Is My West Virginia," words and
music by Iris Bell, "West Virginia,
My Home Sweet Home," words and
music by Julian G. Hearne, Jr.,
"The West Virginia Hills," words by
David King and music by H. E. Engle

Motto
Montani Semper Liberi
(Mountaineers Are Always Free)

Population
(2014 Census) 1,850,326
Ranked 37th state

Entered the Union
June 20, 1863, as the 35th state

Capital
Charleston

Discover West Virginia

With an average altitude of 1,500 feet above sea level, West Virginia is the highest of any U.S. state east of the Mississippi River. This is why the state's nickname is "the Mountain State." It boasts spectacular scenery, beautiful farms, and misty rolling hills. West Virginia also has a rich history and culture that makes visiting the state a rewarding and memorable experience.

West Virginia separated from the state of Virginia during the Civil War. A series of disagreements between the eastern and western parts of Virginia caused the separation. The people of western Virginia felt unfairly taxed and believed that they were receiving few benefits. In addition, many West Virginians were opposed to slave-owning, while wealthy eastern planters owned the majority of slaves in the state.

The capital of West Virginia is Charleston. It is located in Kanawha County, where the Elk and the Kanawha Rivers meet. When Charleston was established in 1794, the total population was 35. It is now the largest city in the state. Charleston is referred to as both the "most northern" of southern cities and the "most southern" of northern cities in the United States. The city has many historic buildings and grand mansions. Many of these landmarks date back to the late 1800s. Downtown Charleston draws many tourists with its entertainment, shops, and trolley-bus rides. Like all of the other large West Virginia cities, Charleston is located in a river valley, where the land is flat. West Virginia's other major cities are Huntington, Wheeling, Parkersburg, and Morgantown.

The Land

General Thomas "Stonewall" Jackson is one of West Virginia's best-known sons. He fought for the Confederacy during the Civil War. A statue in front of the state capitol commemorates him.

West Virginia is divided into **55 counties**.

Traveling ministers, called **circuit riders**, brought religion to isolated settlers of the Appalachian Mountains.

Beginnings

Located in the middle of the Appalachian Mountains, West Virginia is the most mountainous state east of the Rocky Mountains. The state's unusual boundaries, created by mountains and rivers, give it the shape of a pan with two large handles. This shape inspired one of West Virginia's nicknames, the Panhandle State.

West Virginia is known for its unique **rural** mountain culture. Since their mountain location was quite isolated, early West Virginians developed a local culture that was not influenced by neighboring populations. Many of these mountain traditions, such as folk songs and storytelling, still exist today.

European settlement in West Virginia began with German settlers around present-day Shepherdstown. These German settlers made their way into the area of West Virginia around 1727. By the late 1700s, the eastern part of the state was already well established with various towns. The western part of the state took longer to develop due to many disagreements over property rights involving Native Americans as well as competing land grant companies.

The Battle of Shepherdstown, near the Potomac River, was a conflict between Union and Confederate forces in the Civil War. It was such a difficult battle on both sides that it stopped the South's push into Maryland.

Where is WEST VIRGINIA?

W est Virginia is bordered by Pennsylvania and Maryland to the north. Virginia is to the east and the south. Kentucky and Ohio are to the west. The Ohio River forms the border between Ohio and West Virginia. The Potomac River forms part of West Virginia's northern border with Maryland. The Potomac then flows southeast past Washington, D.C., and into Chesapeake Bay.

OHIO

INDIANA

United States Map

West Virginia

Alaska   Hawai'i

KENTUCKY

MAP LEGEND

⬜ West Virginia

☆ Capital City

● Town

▲ Seneca Caverns

🌲 Monongahela Forest

⬜ Bordering States

N

SCALE   0   25 miles

1 Charleston

Located in the Allegheny Mountains, Charleston is the state's largest city. Charleston grew around Fort Lee, which was built by colonists in 1788. Charleston was officially founded in 1794. It became the state's permanent capital in 1885. Today, visitors can experience the Culture Center and State Museum.

2 Harpers Ferry

Harpers Ferry is a living historic town where visitors step back in time to experience Civil War era characters and atmosphere at the confluence of the Potomac and Shenandoah Rivers. The city is layered with events that influenced U.S. history, including witnessing the arrival of the first successful U.S. railroad.

PENNSYLVANIA

WEST VIRGINIA

2 Harpers Ferry

3

4

1
⭐ Charleston

VIRGINIA

3 Seneca Caverns

The limestone bed of the Seneca Caverns was formed more than 460 million years ago. The Seneca Native Americans used the caves for shelter, storage, and special ceremonies. Today, guided tours explore up to 165 feet below the entrance. Beautiful minerals and gems stand out among the dirt, mud, and rocks.

4 Monongahela Forest

With elevations ranging from 1,000 feet to 4,863 feet above sea level, the Monongahela National Forest provides visitors with beautiful vistas, peaceful country roads, wildlife, and the highest mountain peaks in the state. It has a wide variety of both plants and animals, making it one of the most ecologically diverse forests in the country.

Land Features

All of West Virginia lies within the geographic region known as the Appalachian Mountain System. This region extends from Canada to Alabama. The state is further divided into two separate regions. These are the Allegheny Plateau and the Appalachian Ridge.

The Appalachian Ridge is made up of long mountain ridges, which are covered in forests. The Blue Ridge Mountains form the eastern edge of the Appalachian Ridge and are visible from the Eastern Panhandle. The Allegheny Plateau stretches from the Mohawk Valley in New York to the Cumberland Plateau in southern West Virginia.

Seneca Rocks

The Seneca Rocks formation rises nearly 900 feet above the North Fork River. It is one of West Virginia's most visited natural sites.

Appalachian Mountains

The Appalachian Mountains are thought to be among the oldest mountains in the world. This mountain system extends almost 2,000 miles from Labrador and New Brunswick in Canada southwest to Alabama.

New River

The New River, anything but new, has been flowing for more than 300 million years. Geologists believe that it is the oldest river in North America. The Grandview Overlook offers a spectacular view of this waterway.

Blackwater Falls

Blackwater Falls State Park features a waterfall that drops almost 60 feet. This waterfall was named because acid in the water gives it a dark color. The acid comes from tree needles that have fallen into the water.

Climate

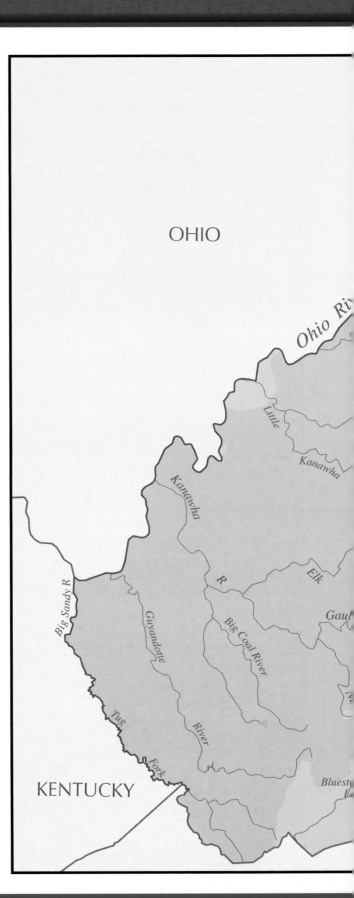

Much of West Virginia lies on the Allegheny Plateau. At the highest point of the plateau, the weather is severe and can change suddenly. Dense fogs can collect, and fierce winds often blow. West Virginia is often humid.

Average January temperatures in West Virginia range from 28° Fahrenheit to 38°F. Average July temperatures vary from 68°F to 76°F. Average annual temperatures range from 56°F in the southwest to 48°F in more mountainous areas with a higher elevation.

Average Annual Precipitation Across West Virginia

Precipitation varies across even a small state like West Virginia. What features of West Virginia's geography do you think contribute to this variation?

LEGEND

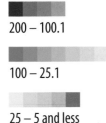

Average Annual Precipitation (in inches) 1961–1990

200 – 100.1

100 – 25.1

25 – 5 and less

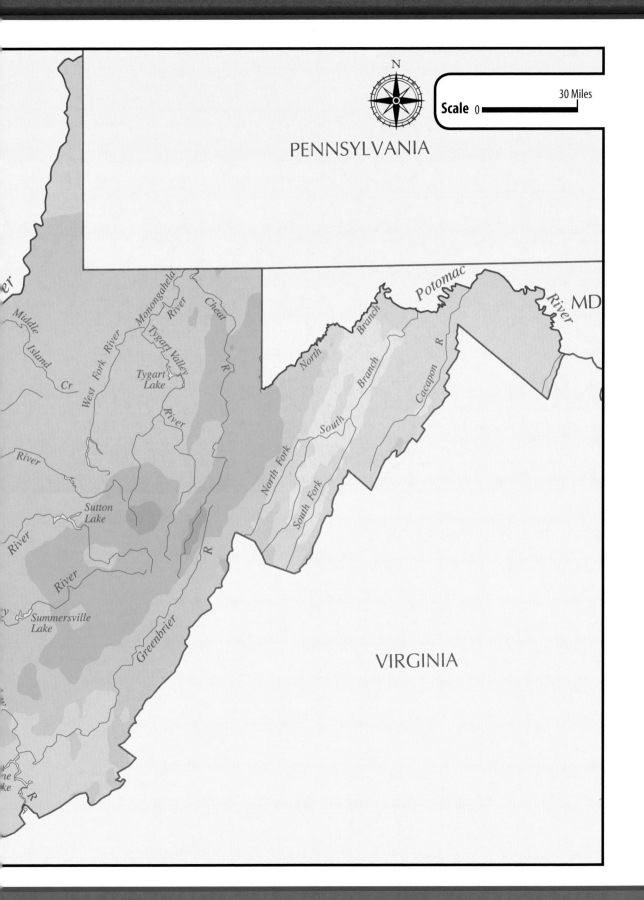

PENNSYLVANIA

MD

Potomac

River

Monongahela

River

Cheat

Middle

Island

West Fork River

Tygart Valley

Tygart
Lake

R

North

Branch

South

Branch

Cacapon R

Cr

River

River

North Fork

South

River

Sutton
Lake

South Fork

River

Summersville
Lake

R

Greenbrier

River

VIRGINIA

R

N

Scale 0 ▬▬▬▬▬▬▬ 30 Miles

Many of West Virginia's coal mines utilize a mining method called "mountaintop removal." In this type of coal mining, a mountaintop is cut away to expose much of the rock and minerals below.

Nature's Resources

West Virginia has many natural resources. It is among the nation's leading sources of **bituminous coal**, producing more than 140 million tons per year. Stone, cement, salt, and oil are also important resources for the state.

The oil and gas industry in West Virginia is linked to the salt industry. In the early 1800s, oil and gas were of little importance. Salt workers in the Kanawha Valley often struck oil or gas while drilling for salt. They thought it was a nuisance. Once the value of oil and natural gas as fuels was recognized, petroleum and gas production in the region boomed. For many years, West Virginia was the largest producer of natural gas east of the Mississippi River. The state still produces large amounts of natural gas in the Appalachian Basin.

West Virginia has large reserves of rock salt. It is extracted from the ground, instead of from salt water.

West Virginia's natural gas deposits are primarily found in the west-central region. Fracking, a technique that pushes fluid into the ground, is the primary way natural gas is extracted in the state.

Vegetation

Compared to mountain ranges in the western United States, the Appalachians have deep soil in which many plants flourish. In Kanawha State Forest, visitors can find a wide variety of trees and plants. They include 23 species of wild orchids. West Virginia is the habitat of many flowering bushes, such as laurel, hepatica, wild geranium, and black-eyed Susan. Oak, maple, birch, and pine trees all grow in West Virginia.

Another region that stands out for its fertile soil and fine climate is the valley of the New River. Over millions of years, the New River has moved many tons of rich **sediment** into its lower valley. As a result, the soil along the valley floor is ideal for growing plants and produces an abundant amount of lush vegetation.

Oak Tree

Oak trees lose their leaves each winter. Smaller oak trees usually grow 20 to 30 feet tall, and large ones can be as high as 100 feet tall.

Maple Tree

West Virginia made the sugar maple its official state tree in 1949. Sugar maples provide valuable timber and maple syrup.

Sunflowers

About 18 kinds of sunflowers grow in West Virginia. The plants may grow several feet high.

Soapwort

Soapwort is a plant common in the summer. The flowers are pink or white. The leaves froth like soap when they are crushed.

Wildlife

In the area around Bluestone State Park, blue herons, kingfishers, bobcats, foxes, and wild turkeys can be seen in the woods. Many kinds of large mammals have disappeared from the state, but deer and black bears can still be found in the high country. Trout, bass, and pike swim in West Virginia's streams and rivers.

West Virginia has many different kinds of birds. Loons, ducks, and geese are **migratory** species. Quails, woodcocks, owls, eagles, and hawks also fly in West Virginia's skies. The songs of the cardinal, wood thrush, brown thrasher, and scarlet tanager can be heard throughout the state.

Timber Rattlesnake

Timber rattlesnakes are present across most of the United States. They live in the high woods and rugged mountains of West Virginia. These **venomous** snakes will not pursue or attack a person unless threatened or provoked.

Opossum

Opossums are found across West Virginia. Excellent tree climbers, they can use their tail as a fifth limb. These scavengers eat whatever is around.

Northern Cardinal

The cardinal was made West Virginia's official state bird in 1949. The males are deep red with black masks. Cardinals are small, measuring about 8 inches.

Brook Trout

The brook trout has been West Virginia's official state fish since 1973. The brook trout thrives in cool, spring-fed streams and lakes. It cannot survive in warmer water.

Economy

Cass Scenic Railroad State Park

Cass Scenic Railroad State Park is located in Pocahontas County. The heritage railroad, with its steam-driven locomotives, stretches for 11 miles.

Tourism

Tourism is very important to West Virginia's economy. The state's natural beauty attracts visitors from across the country. There are plenty of outdoor activities to enjoy in West Virginia's 9 state forests and 35 state parks, including fishing, hunting, river rafting, hiking, camping, and skiing. More than a million acres of West Virginia land are dedicated to parks.

Mineral springs are another popular attraction found throughout the state. The best known are those at Berkeley Springs and White Sulphur Springs. Berkeley Springs is the oldest **spa** in the country.

New River Gorge Bridge

The New River Gorge Bridge is the country's longest single-arch steel bridge. It is 3,030 feet long.

Beckley Exhibition Coal Mine

Visitors to the Beckley Exhibition Coal Mine can explore some of the 1,500 feet of underground passages, ride in an underground coal car, and experience what the lives of West Virginia's rugged miners might have been like in the early 1900s.

Canaan Valley

Canaan Valley is considered to have some of the best skiing in the mid-Atlantic states. The valley has six resorts to accommodate skiers. Snow in the valley often lasts well into the spring.

West Virginia contains an estimated 50 billion tons of usable coal reserves. In 2012, more than 129 million tons of coal extracted from the state's mines.

Primary Industries

Mining and manufacturing are very important in West Virginia. Together, they account for about one-fifth of the state's economy. These two industries have made significant contributions to West Virginia's history as well as its economy.

In 2009, West Virginia mines produced more than 144 million tons of coal. There are coal deposits in 53 of West Virginia's 55 counties. West Virginia also mines limestone. The limestone bedrock **quarried** in the state is rich in calcium carbonate, potassium, and phosphorus. The minerals in West Virginia lime make it an excellent fertilizer for farm pastures and lawns.

Manufacturing areas in West Virginia are along the Kanawha River and the Ohio River, as well as in the cities of Charleston, Huntington, and Wheeling. These areas are responsible for the production of chemicals, glass, **fabricated metals**, high-technology products, and machinery. Some manufacturing in West Virginia makes use of the state's mineral resources as raw materials.

Coal-fired electric power plants accounted for **95.5 percent** of West Virginia's net electricity generation in 2014.

The first **state sales tax** in the United States went into effect in West Virginia on **July 1, 1921**.

Value of Goods and Services (in Millions of Dollars)

Although mining and manufacturing are major industries, in recent decades many types of service industries have become increasingly important in West Virginia. They include stores, hospitals, banks, restaurants, and government agencies that provide services to people. How would a pie chart showing West Virginia's economy in the 1800s look different from today's chart?

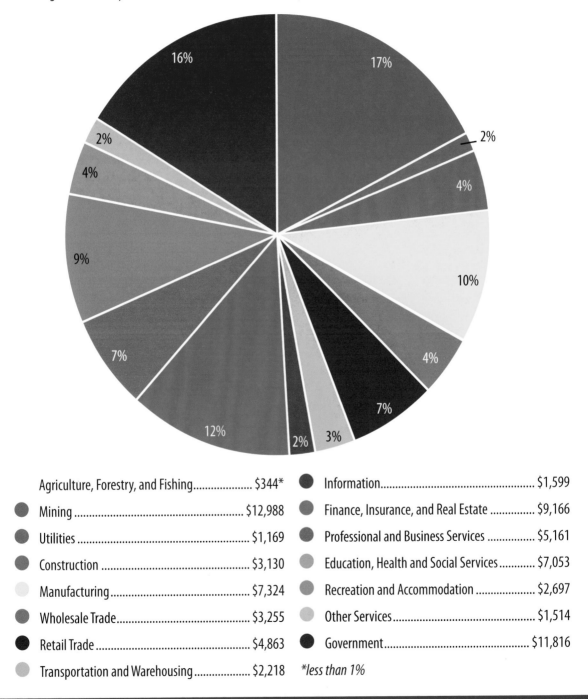

Agriculture, Forestry, and Fishing.................... $344*

Mining $12,988

Utilities $1,169

Construction $3,130

Manufacturing.. $7,324

Wholesale Trade... $3,255

Retail Trade $4,863

Transportation and Warehousing................... $2,218

Information... $1,599

Finance, Insurance, and Real Estate $9,166

Professional and Business Services $5,161

Education, Health and Social Services............ $7,053

Recreation and Accommodation $2,697

Other Services.. $1,514

Government.. $11,816

*less than 1%

West Virginia's eastern panhandle is one of the prime apple-growing regions in the country. In 2013, 2,260,000 bushels of apples were harvested in the state.

Goods and Services

Large fruit orchards in West Virginia's Eastern Panhandle grow apples and peaches. West Virginia does not have much flat land for crops, but hay, wheat, oats, soybeans, corn, and tobacco are grown. Farmers also produce dairy products, and they raise **broiler chickens**, turkeys, and cattle.

West Virginia is a global hub for chemical development. Major companies, including DuPont and Bayer, have facilities in the state. Chemical development employs about 13,500 people state-wide.

West Virginia's glass country can be found in the rolling hills of the Tri-State region, where Ohio, Kentucky, and West Virginia meet. Dozens of companies make beautiful glass products using the state's sand deposits. Many **artisans** in this region make handmade and blown glassware and offer glassmaking demonstrations to visitors.

Glass making, from windows to marbles, is one of the state's oldest industries. It was established in the Wheeling area in the 1830s.

Many West Virginia workers have jobs in the service sector. Some of these jobs are with the government, in health-care facilities, and in public transit. Tourism is an important part of the service industry in West Virginia. More than 65,000 West Virginians are employed in the tourist industry. Some of these people work in restaurants, in hotels, and at tourist attractions.

Although the rocky Appalachians limited movement within West Virginia for centuries, modern railroad lines now extend about 2,500 miles throughout the state.

Grave Creek, near Moundsville, West Virginia, was built by the Adena culture. The mounds were used for ceremonial and religious purposes and were often at the heart of the local community.

Native Americans

The first people in West Virginia were prehistoric Native Americans. These early hunters lived in the area between 8,000 and 10,000 years ago. **Archaeologists** have found their stone tools in the Kanawha and Ohio Valleys. These prehistoric people were often on the move and never settled permanently in the area.

Later, several different cultures settled in West Virginia's Northern and Eastern Panhandles. There, archaeologists have uncovered tools, pottery, and ceremonial burial grounds. Most of these remains are from the Adena and Hopewell cultures. The people built large ceremonial mounds, for which they earned the name Mound Builders.

The Grave Creek Mound, in Marshall County, is the largest mound in the United States. It is 62 feet high and 240 feet in diameter. Archaeologists believe that it was built between 250 and 150 BC.

By the 1600s, the Lenape, or Delaware, and the Shawnee had moved into West Virginia. At about the same time, the Iroquois Confederacy began coming to the area. The Iroquois Confederacy was an **alliance** of five Iroquois-speaking nations. They are the Mohawk, Oneida, Onondaga, Cayuga, and Seneca groups. In 1722, the Tuscarora joined the Iroquois Confederacy, and it became known as the Six Nations.

European exploration and settlement forced many Native Americans west. As a result of this forced migration, there was much tension and bloodshed in the 1600s and 1700s. By the mid-1700s, the Iroquois began to give up their land claims in West Virginia through a series of **treaties**.

Although few of West Virginia's Native American groups remain, their influence can still be seen in such artifacts as petroglyphs, which are drawings on rock.

Exploring the Land

It is thought that the first person of European descent to see what is now West Virginia was John Lederer. Lederer and his group reached the top of the Blue Ridge Mountains, which are along the border between present-day Virginia and West Virginia. At the time, Lederer was exploring for Sir William Berkeley, the governor of the British colony of Virginia. Lederer made a total of three trips to the Blue Ridge Mountains between 1669 and 1670.

Timeline of Settlement

Early Exploration and Colonization

1669 John Lederer and his companions become the first people of European descent to view what is now West Virginia.

1669 French explorer René-Robert Cavelier, sieur de La Salle, explores the Ohio River.

1671 Thomas Batts and Robert Fallam claim for Great Britain land that is now part of West Virginia.

1607 Great Britain establishes the colony of Virginia, with its first settlement along the coast at Jamestown.

1722 The Iroquois surrender land south of the Ohio River, including areas in the Eastern Panhandle.

Colony Established

The French and the British battled for control of the region for nearly 100 years. The discovery of the New River in 1671 was a turning point for the British. With access to the great river, the British could expand their power by laying claim to the entire Ohio Valley. The expedition that discovered this ancient river was called the Batts and Fallam Expedition. The discovery allowed fur traders and explorers to move farther west, into Virginia's wilderness.

The British eventually defeated the French in the French and Indian War. The war lasted from 1754 to 1763. The British then gained complete control over the area that is now West Virginia.

1783 The American Revolutionary War, which began in 1775, ends in the creation of the United States.

1788 Virginia, including land that is now West Virginia, becomes the 10th state to ratify, or approve, the new U.S. Constitution.

1859 Abolitionist John Brown unsuccessfully raids Harpers Ferry.

1732 German, Welsh, Scottish, and Irish pioneers settle in western Virginia.

Statehood and Civil War

1731 Morgan Morgan establishes the first settlement in what is now West Virginia, near Bunker Hill.

1863 During the Civil War, West Virginia is admitted to the Union as the 35th state, separate from Virginia.

Settlements and Conflict

1865 The African American 55th Massachusetts Regiment marches through Charleston. Soon after, the South surrenders, ending the Civil War.

Tobacco became an important crop in the New World shortly after the founding of Jamestown, Virginia.

The First Settlers

The area now known as the Eastern Panhandle attracted West Virginia's early settlers. General Daniel Morgan was one of West Virginia's first settlers. Both Morgantown and Morgan County were named in his family's honor.

The Shenandoah Valley was a major southern migration route for Scottish, Irish, and German settlers. Many people from these cultural groups first went to Pennsylvania and New Jersey when they arrived from Europe. Later, they or their descendants moved southwest into what is now West Virginia.

Many settlers built homes along West Virginia's rivers, but a few settled on the Allegheny Plateau. By 1800, West Virginia's population had risen to 78,000. Most West Virginia families at this time made their living by farming. Settlement in the region continued to grow as natural resources, such as coal and oil, were discovered.

General Daniel Morgan was a leading figure in the American Revolutionary War. After the war, he settled in what would become West Virginia and served in the United States House of Representatives.

During the nineteenth century, Parkersburg grew to become a hub of industry in West Virginia. The city served as a transportation and medical center for Union forces during the Civil War.

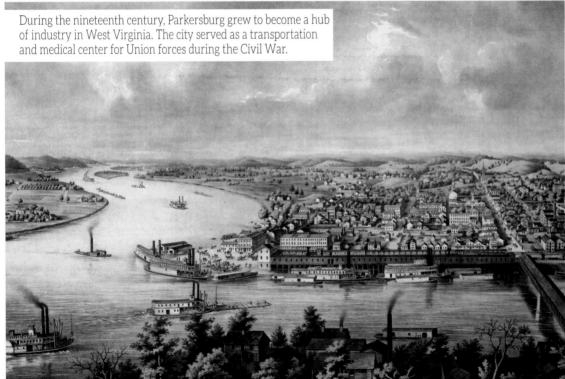

History Makers

Many notable people from West Virginia have contributed to the development of the 35th state as well as the rest of the country. The residents of West Virginia have historically shown independent spirits. Before and after the region split from Virginia in 1863, the Mountain State has been home to prominent military leaders, educators, social and political activists, and aviation pioneers.

Chief Logan (c. 1725–1780)

Chief Logan, a Cayuga Native American, lived in the Ohio River Valley. Colonists murdered his family in an attack in 1774. Logan retaliated, helping to start the last war in which colonists fought on the side of Great Britain before the American Revolutionary War. Logan refused to take part in peace negotiations and is remembered for his speech known as "Logan's Lament."

Stonewall Jackson (1824–1863)

Thomas Jonathan "Stonewall" Jackson was born in 1824 in Clarksburg, Virginia, now West Virginia. He did not support slavery. However, when Virginia joined the Confederacy at the beginning of the Civil War, he became a general in the Confederate army. A celebrated commander, Jackson earned his nickname on the battlefields, where he stood "like a stone wall." He died in 1863, shot accidentally by his own men.

Booker T. Washington (1856–1915)

Washington was born a slave in Virginia in 1856. After he was freed, he moved with his family to West Virginia and worked hard to educate himself. Later, he led a school for African Americans in Tuskegee, Alabama. Booker T. Washington, who focused on improving the position of freed slaves in the country, became a powerful political activist.

Walter Reuther (1907–1970)

Born in Wheeling, Reuther became a prominent U.S. labor union leader. A factory worker from the age of 16, he helped organize sit-down strikes in the late 1930s. Reuther served as president of the United Automobile Workers, or UAW, from 1946 until his death in 1970.

Chuck Yeager (1923–)

Charles "Chuck" Elwood Yeager became the first person to fly faster than the speed of sound. On October 14, 1947, he broke the sound barrier while flying the experimental Bell X-1. He also became the first person to fly at more than twice the speed of sound. Yeager was born at Myra in Lincoln County.

Nearly 18 percent of West Virginians are over the age of 65.

More than 50,000 people call West Virginia's capital of Charleston home.

The People Today

West Virginia is the 37th most populated state in the country. There are more than 1.8 million people living in the state. About 95 percent of West Virginians are of European heritage, while almost 4 percent are African American.

In 2010, West Virginia had an average of 77.1 people per square mile. West Virginia has the highest **median age** in the country. Many residents of West Virginia live the Eastern Panhandle, one of the most densely populated regions of the state. West Virginia's largest county by population is Kanawha, which has more than 190,000 residents.

The state has, in recent years, seen little change in population. West Virginia has experienced a low **birthrate**, as well as migration out of the state. West Virginia's average birthrate of about 11 births per 1,000 people is below the national average of 14 per 1,000 people.

Unlike many U.S. states, West Virginia has seen an overall **decline** in its population since **1950**.

Q What impact might a drop in population have on the state's government and economy?

At 292 feet tall, the West Virginia state capitol is the tallest building in the state.

State Government

West Virginia's government is divided into three branches. They are the executive, the legislative, and the judicial branches. The executive branch carries out state laws. The legislative branch makes new laws and changes existing ones. The judicial branch enforces and interprets the laws. All of the high-level officeholders in the three branches are elected by the people of West Virginia.

The executive branch is headed by a governor, who is elected to a four-year term. The governor is responsible for proposing the state budget, for appointing state department directors, and for signing bills into laws. The state's legislature has a Senate with 34 members and a House of Delegates with 100 members. West Virginia adopted three state songs in 1963. A fourth state song was added in 2014. "West Virginia Hills" is sung by the people of West Virginia to remember their origin and the remarkable features of their state.

The Supreme Court of Appeals is West Virginia's highest court. It has five judges, who are called justices and who serve 12-year terms. Lower courts in the state include circuit courts and magistrate courts.

The design of the West Virginia state capitol chambers was well-received. It was the inspiration for the U.S. Supreme Court.

Before becoming governor in 2013, Earl Ray Tomblin served in the West Virginia State Senate for more than 17 years.

West Virginia's state song is
"West Virginia Hills."

Oh, the West Virginia hills!
How majestic and how grand,
With their summits bathed in glory,
Like our Prince Immanuel's Land!
Is it any wonder then,
That my heart with rapture thrills,
As I stand once more with loved ones
On those West Virginia hills?
Chorus:
Oh, the hills, beautiful hills,
How I love those West Virginia hills!
If o'er sea o'er land I roam,
Still I'll think of happy home,
And my friends among
the West Virginia hills.

* excerpted

The Mountain State Forest Festival offers many activities for visitors each autumn. There are forestry, woodwork, and photography exhibits, lumberjack competitions, arts and crafts, and parades.

Celebrating Culture

Until the 1890s, people of German and Scots-Irish heritage were the most numerous ethnic groups in West Virginia. At that time, the industrial expansion of the state attracted many European immigrants. Today, about 1 percent of the people of West Virginia are foreign-born. Many of West Virginia's farm families are descended from early settlers and have owned their land for generations.

Deep in the heart of the Potomac Valley's Randolph County is a small community established by Swiss immigrants. They named their town Helvetia in honor of their homeland. Helvetia is the word for "Switzerland" in Latin. Many of the town's buildings were modeled after the architecture of Switzerland, and a Swiss-German **dialect** can still be heard in the streets.

The city of Elkins hosts one of West Virginia's oldest and largest festivals. The Mountain State Forest Festival celebrates the important role that natural resources play in the state's economic development. The festival sees more than 75,000 visitors in attendance each year.

West Virginia recognizes and celebrates the cultural heritage of the state's coal-mining industry. Since coal was discovered in southern West Virginia along the Coal River in 1742, more than 4 billion tons have been mined from these historic coalfields.

In the town of Augusta, the Augusta Heritage Center teaches old-time banjo playing. The banjo is a popular traditional folk instrument in West Virginia. The Vandalia Gathering in Charleston honors the state's ethnic heritage. Irish, Swiss, Scottish, and Appalachian styles of dance take place. Banjo, guitar, and dulcimer musicians compete for prizes.

The National Coal Heritage Area is spread across 13 counties in the Appalachian Mountains of West Virginia. Many structures have been preserved along the Coal Heritage Trail for guests to experience.

The Vandalia Gathering is put on by the West Virginia Division of Culture and history. It celebrates traditional folklife, including Appalachian dulcimer music.

Kathy Mattea blends traditional folk music, bluegrass, country, and Celtic styles to create her own unique sound.

Arts and Entertainment

There has always been a love of bluegrass and country music in West Virginia. The music capital of the state is Wheeling, where the live-radio country music show *Jamboree USA* is broadcast to devoted listeners. It is the second-oldest live radio show in the U.S.

West Virginia's strong country music roots have produced many singing stars. Grammy-winning Kathy Mattea has recorded more than a dozen studio albums. She has enjoyed enormous fan support, along with many number-one hits.

One of West Virginia's most famous writers is Pearl S. Buck, who won the Pulitzer Prize in 1932 for her book *The Good Earth*. Buck also won the Nobel Prize for Literature. She was the first woman from the United States to win both awards. Buck was born and raised in Hillsboro, which is part of West Virginia's Pocahontas County.

Morgan Spurlock, the documentary filmmaker best known for *Super Size Me*, was born in Parkersburg, West Virginia.

The **Victoria Theater**, in Wheeling, West Virginia, began operation in 1904. It is the **oldest continually-operating theater** in the state.

In June, the Greenbrier Valley Festival of the Arts is held in Lewisburg. Local artists and musicians gather to present a weekend of world-class entertainment. The Eastern Panhandle is very proud of its history. Each spring the region celebrates the past with large festivals, such as the Mountain Heritage Arts and Crafts Festival. Many of the most important playwrights from the United States are showcased at the month-long Contemporary American Theater Festival at Shepherd College in Shepherdstown.

Pearl S. Buck spent much of her young adult life in China. Much of her writing concentrates on Eastern themes and the relationship between East and West.

Actress Jennifer Garner grew up in West Virginia. She is perhaps best-known for her role in the television series *Alias*. Garner went on to appear in several films, including *The Invention of Lying* in 2009, along with *Alexander and the Terrible, Horrible, No Good, Very Bad Day*.

Jennifer Garner grew up in Charleston, West Virginia. In 2006, she won a People's Choice Award for Favorite Female Action Star and Favorite Female Television Star.

Seneca Rocks is one of the most challenging rock climbing areas in the state.

Sports and Recreation

Race-car driving in the Shenandoah Valley is very popular, even with movie stars. Both Paul Newman and Tom Cruise paid regular visits to West Virginia's Summit Point Raceway. It is considered one of the most challenging auto racing tracks in the nation. The raceway hosts Sports Car Club of America events for professional and amateur auto racing, as well as motorcycle and go-cart races.

West Virginia is home to a number of popular yet unusual sports. Rock climbers from around the nation come to the Potomac Highlands to climb the incredible sandstone formations known as the Seneca Rocks. Wood chopping is another unusual sport that is practiced in West Virginia. A back-breaking competition is held yearly at the Webster County Woodchopping Festival. The rugged and difficult life of the lumberjack is celebrated by competitors from around the world.

Mary Lou Retton, born in Fairmont in 1968, won five medals at the 1984 Summer Olympics. She was the first U.S. athlete to win the **individual all-around gold medal** in Olympic gymnastics.

The first bareknuckle world heavyweight **boxing** championship was held on June 1, 1880, near Colliers, and lasted 85 rounds.

West Virginia has excellent white-water rafting along some of its wilder rivers. Sometimes called the Grand Canyon of the East, the New River Gorge National Park is a popular tourist attraction. In the Gauley River National Recreational Area, there are some difficult rapids, whose names include "Heaven Help You" and "Lost Paddle."

West Virginia has one of the largest hardwood forests in the nation. The forest supports a lively lumberjack culture and competitions.

Both the New River and Gauley River offer multiple spots for exciting white-water rafting.

Get To Know
WEST VIRGINIA

THE WORLD'S FIRST ELECTRIC RAILROAD WAS BUILT IN WEST VIRGINIA IN 1879.

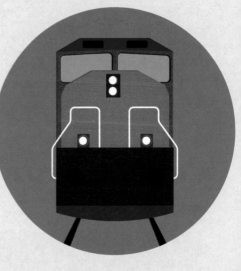

HORSE RACING HAS BEEN A WEST VIRGINIAN PASTIME SINCE CHARLES TOWN RACES OPENED IN 1786.

Stone from West Virginia quarries was used in the **Washington Monument**.

The **Cheat Mountain salamander** lives only in West Virginia.

The **monarch butterfly** is West Virginia's official state butterfly.

According to West Virginia state law, it is **illegal** to **nap** on a train.

The Lilly Family Reunion is held each year at Flat Top in Merer County. It is the largest family reunion in the U.S., attracting **10,000** guests each summer

Brain Teasers

What have you learned about West Virginia after reading this book? Test your knowledge by answering these questions. All of the information can be found in the text you just read. The answers are provided below for easy reference.

1 What is the capital of West Virginia?

2 Access to what great river allowed the British to expand their power to the entire Ohio Valley?

3 Who is thought to be the first person of European descent to see what is now West Virginia?

4 On what date did West Virginia become its own state?

5 What are the three branches of West Virginia's state government?

6 What is West Virginia's state bird?

7 What two industries are very important to West Virginia?

8 What is the average altitude of West Virginia?

Key Words

abolitionist: someone who wants to put an end to slavery

alliance: a union

archaeologists: scientists who study early peoples through artifacts and remains

artisans: highly skilled craftspeople

birthrate: the number of births compared to the total population

bituminous coal: a type of soft coal that burns with a smoky flame

broiler chickens: chickens raised for their meat rather than their eggs

dialect: a particular variety of a language, usually specific to a geographic area

fabricated metals: metals that are manufactured, such as steel

median age: in population, the age at which exactly half of the population is older and the other half is younger

migratory: moving from one place to another

quarried: removed as a stone from an excavation pit

rural: relating to the countryside, people who live in the country, or agriculture

sediment: minerals and organic matter that are deposited by water or ice

spa: a resort people go to in order to benefit from the site's mineral-rich waters

treaties: formal agreements between two parties

venomous: containing or producing a poison called venom

Index

American Revolutionary War 29, 31, 32
Appalachian Mountains 6, 7, 11

Blackwater Falls 11
Buck, Pearl S. 40, 41

Canaan Valley 21
Cass Scenic Railroad State Park 20
Charleston 4, 5, 8, 12, 22, 29, 35, 39, 46
Chief Logan 32
Civil War 5, 6, 7, 8, 29, 31, 33
coal 14, 21, 22, 30, 39, 41

Harpers Ferry 8, 29

Jackson, General Thomas "Stonewall" 6, 33

La Salle, René-Robert Cavelier, sieur de 28
Lederer, John 28, 46

Mattea, Kathy 40
Monongahela Forest 9
Morgan, Daniel 29, 30, 31, 40
Mountain State Forest Festival 38

Native American 7, 9, 27, 32
New River 11, 16, 21, 29, 43, 46

Reuther, Walter 33

Seneca Caverns 9
Shepherdstown 7, 41

tobacco 24, 30

Washington, Booker T. 33

Yeager, Chuck 33

Log on to www.av2books.com

AV^2 by Weigl brings you media enhanced books that support active learning. Go to www.av2books.com, and enter the special code found on page 2 of this book. You will gain access to enriched and enhanced content that supplements and complements this book. Content includes video, audio, weblinks, quizzes, a slide show, and activities.

AV^2 Online Navigation

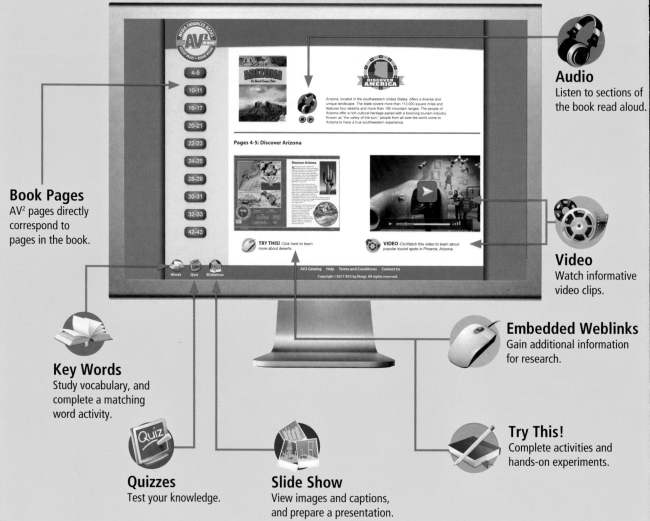

Audio
Listen to sections of the book read aloud.

Book Pages
AV^2 pages directly correspond to pages in the book.

Video
Watch informative video clips.

Embedded Weblinks
Gain additional information for research.

Key Words
Study vocabulary, and complete a matching word activity.

Try This!
Complete activities and hands-on experiments.

Quizzes
Test your knowledge.

Slide Show
View images and captions, and prepare a presentation.

AV^2 was built to bridge the gap between print and digital. We encourage you to tell us what you like and what you want to see in the future.

Sign up to be an AV^2 Ambassador at www.av2books.com/ambassador.